SOCIALLY CONSCIOUS
ABSTRACT ART
BY
SEMAIAH N. LUMA

Copyright © 2021 Semaiah N. Luma.

All rights reserved. This book or any portion thereof may not be reproduced or used in any manner whatsoever without the express written permission of the author or the publisher except for the use of brief quotations in a book review.

Published by Space Age Investment Group, LLC., in the U.S.A.

First volume printed, 2021.

Illustration by Semaiah Luma
Book design by Semaiah Luma
Chief Editor by Lakesha Luma

Space Age Investment Group, LLC
Baltimore, Maryland

www.semaiah.com

Table of Contents

Black is Beautiful:	3
U.S.A. Proud:	4
Thank You Nurses:	5
Tiger:	6
Laundry Day (Black):	7
Laundry Day:	8
Save The Earth:	9
Black Lady with Blue Background:	10
Veteran Strong:	11
Black Man is A Man:	12
I Am Beautiful:	13
Brown Lady on a Blanket:	14
2020 Major Events:	15
Beauty Queen:	16
DIVA:	17
Fly High:	18
Flying Into Space:	19
I Voted 2020 (Male):	20
I Voted 2020 (Female):	21
The Smell of Books:	22
Amoung Us:	23
Holidays 2020:	24
We Are All Beautiful Girls:	25
Bright Beauty:	26

Black is Beautiful

I saw a beautiful Black woman on an app called Pinterest and I wanted to incorporate her beauty in my print. This print's message is all Black women are beautiful.

BLACK IS BEAUTIFUL

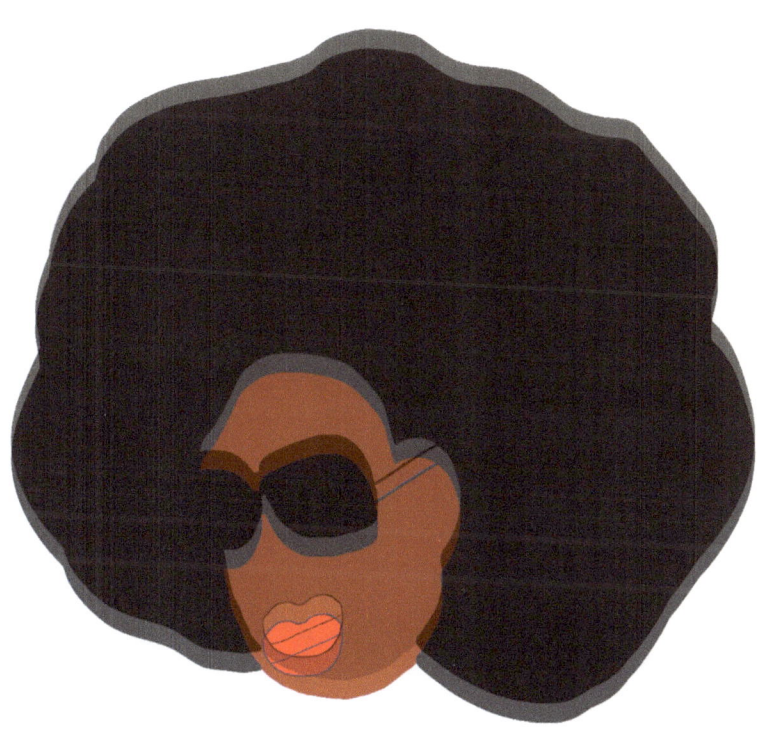

U.S.A. Proud

This print was requested from a Veteran who I met while selling art in a flea market. He explained that he did not see a lot of original art for Veterans or a display of American pride. He felt like the U.S.A. citizens were currently divided and this will remind people that we must work together in this country as U.S. citizens. This print could also remind people to love and respect others despite their race, culture, religion or ethnicity.

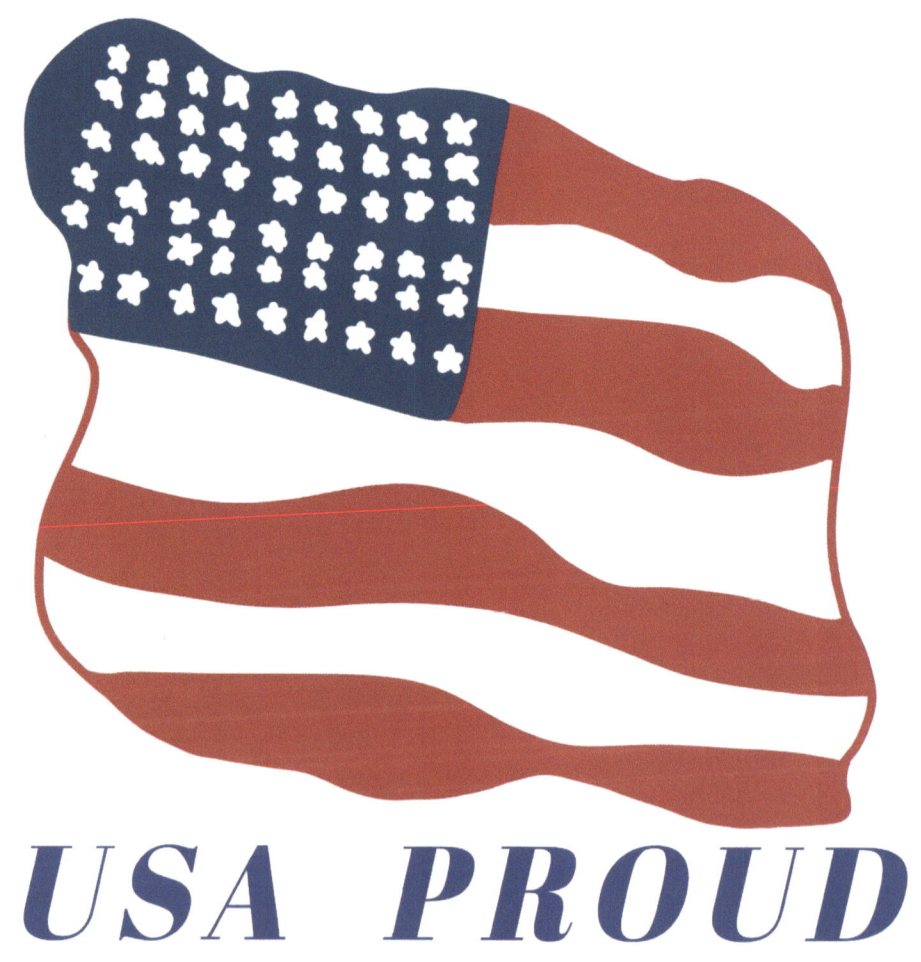

USA PROUD

Thank You Nurses

The year 2020 marked the time of the pandemic. Many frontline workers such as nurses were courageous during this time. They cared for others despite the fact that they could contract the COVID-19 virus. I made this print to show my appreciation towards nurses who care for patients all around the world.

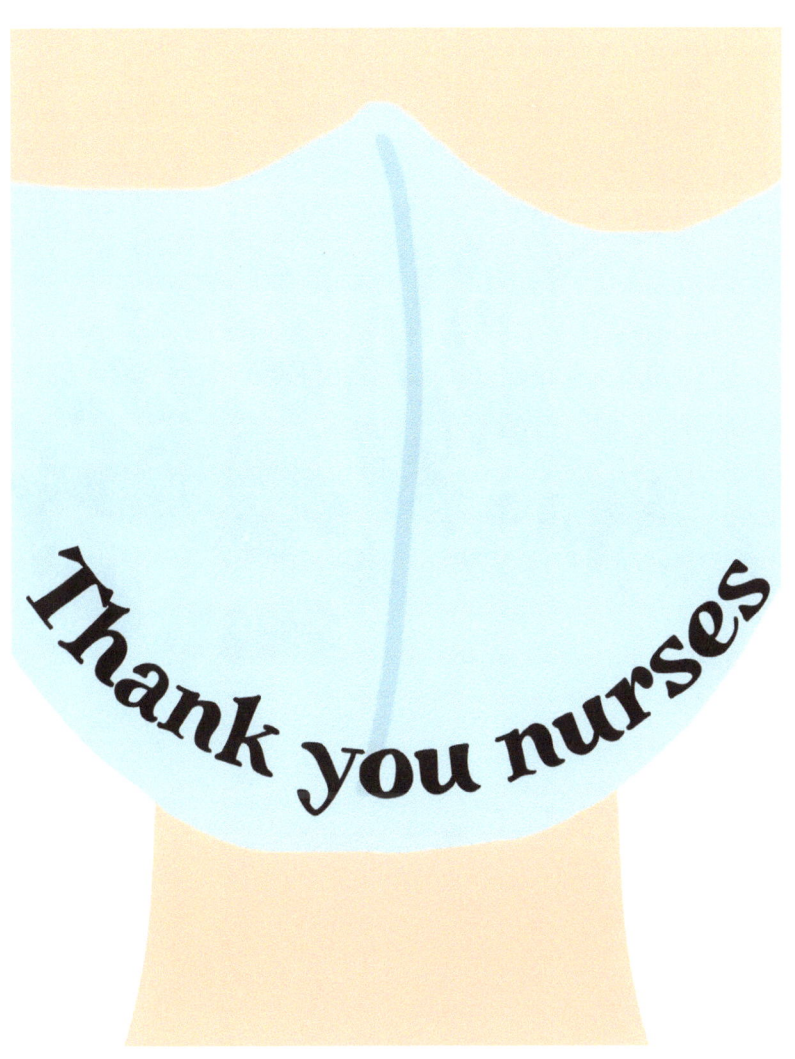

Tiger

This print brings awareness about the fact that tiger's are classified as Endangered. According to the International Union of Conservation of Nature, there are only about 3,500 tigers in the wild around the world.

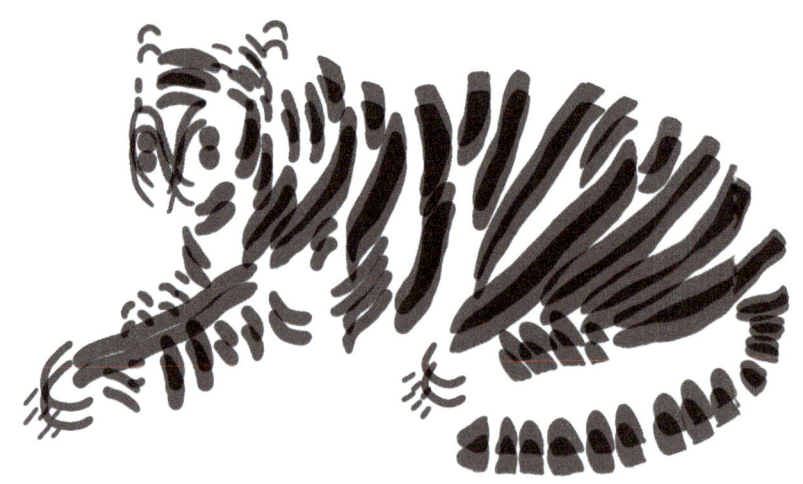

Semaiah L. 2020

Laundry Day (Black)

I have two "Laundry Day" prints and this is the original version. This print represent living in the moment and appreciating the simple things in life. In the past, people actually had time to hang clothes on a line. Over time, I believe people have become so busy that it is hard to enjoy the life's simple treasures.

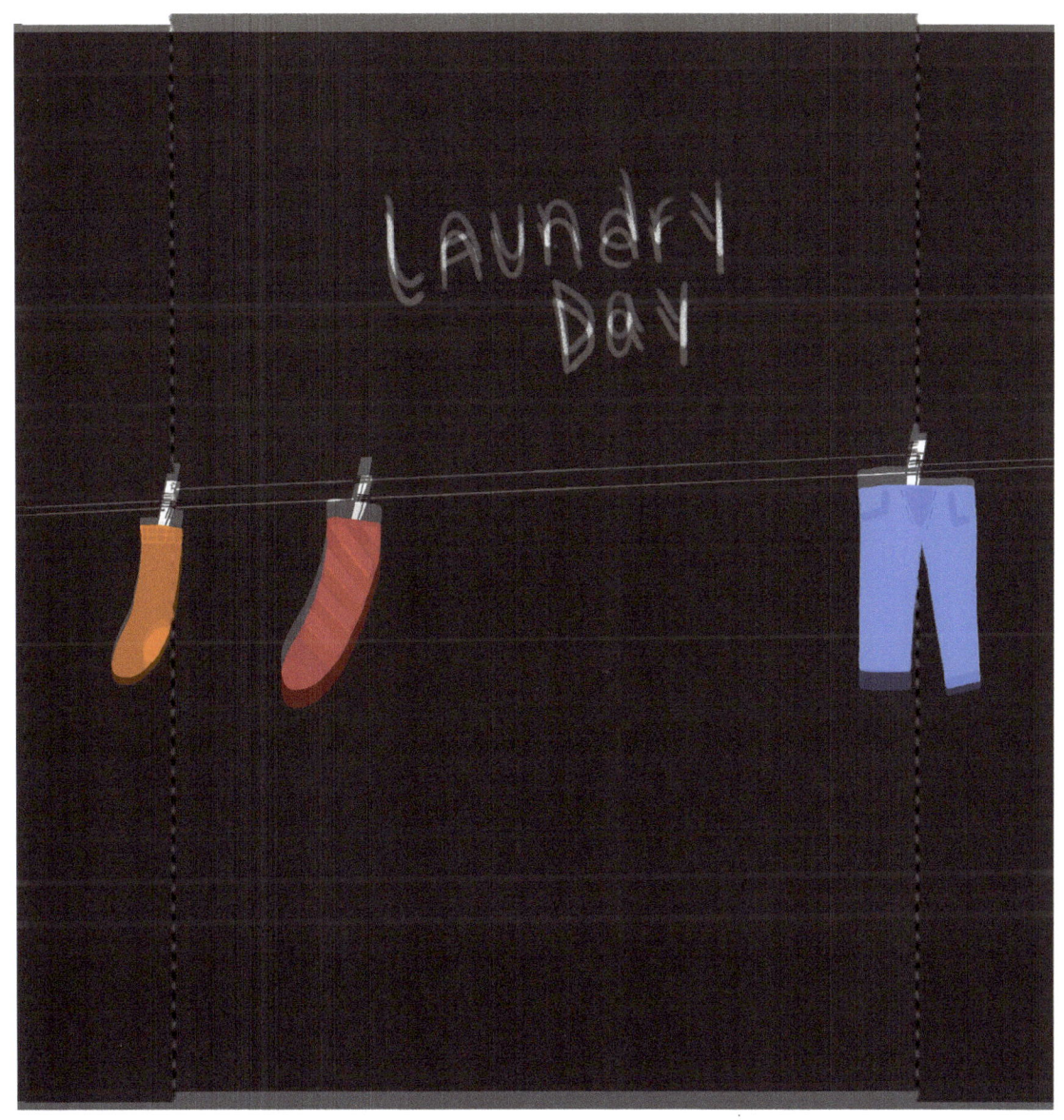

Laundry Day

This is "Laundry Day" number two. This print represent living in the moment and appreciating the simple things in life. In the past, people actually had time to hang clothes on a line. Over time, I believe people have become so busy that it is hard to enjoy the life's simple treasures.

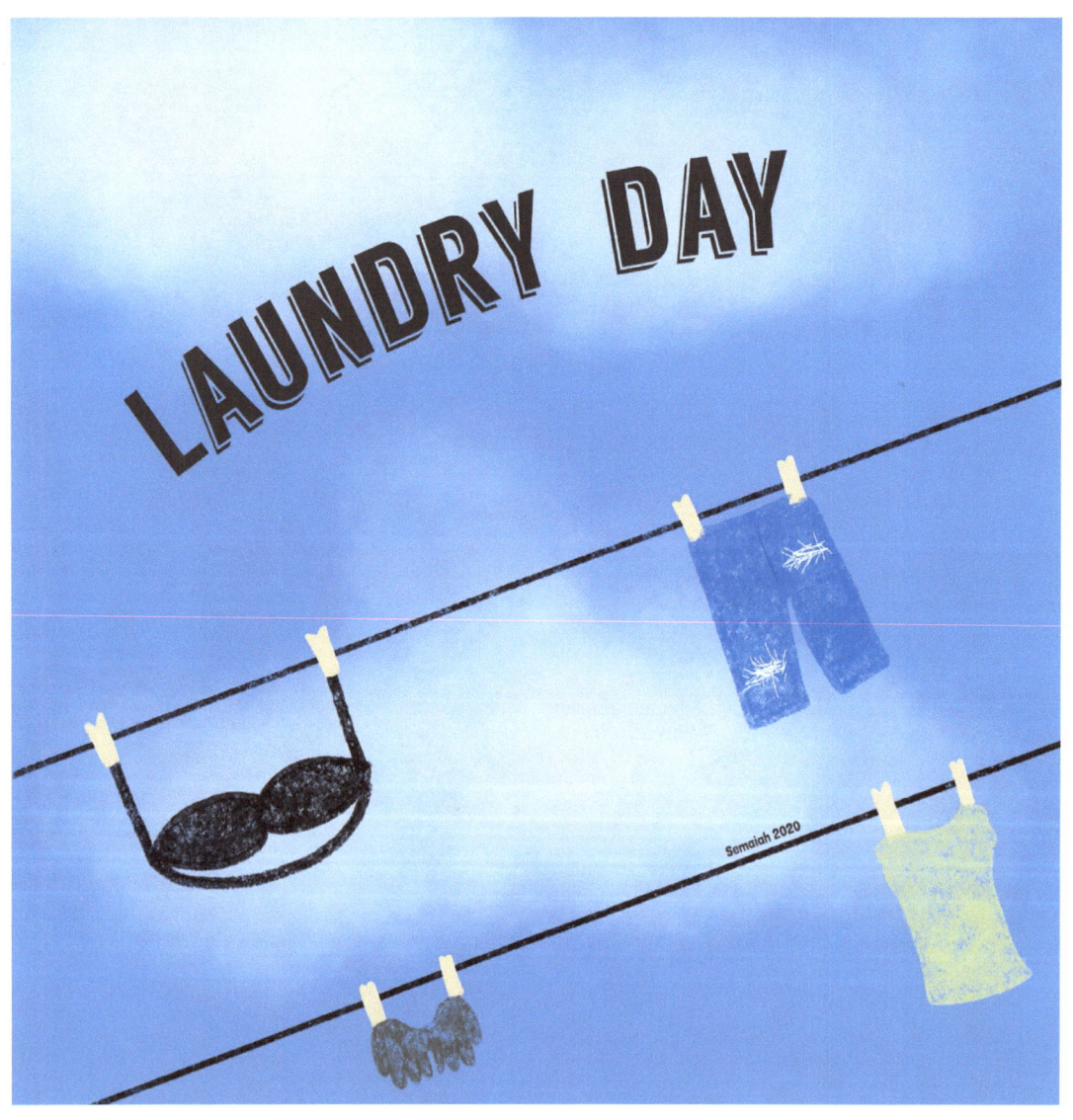

Save The Earth

This print was inspired by the Global Warming happening in our world. I made this print to spread awareness about the importance of recycling and the importance of using solar energy.

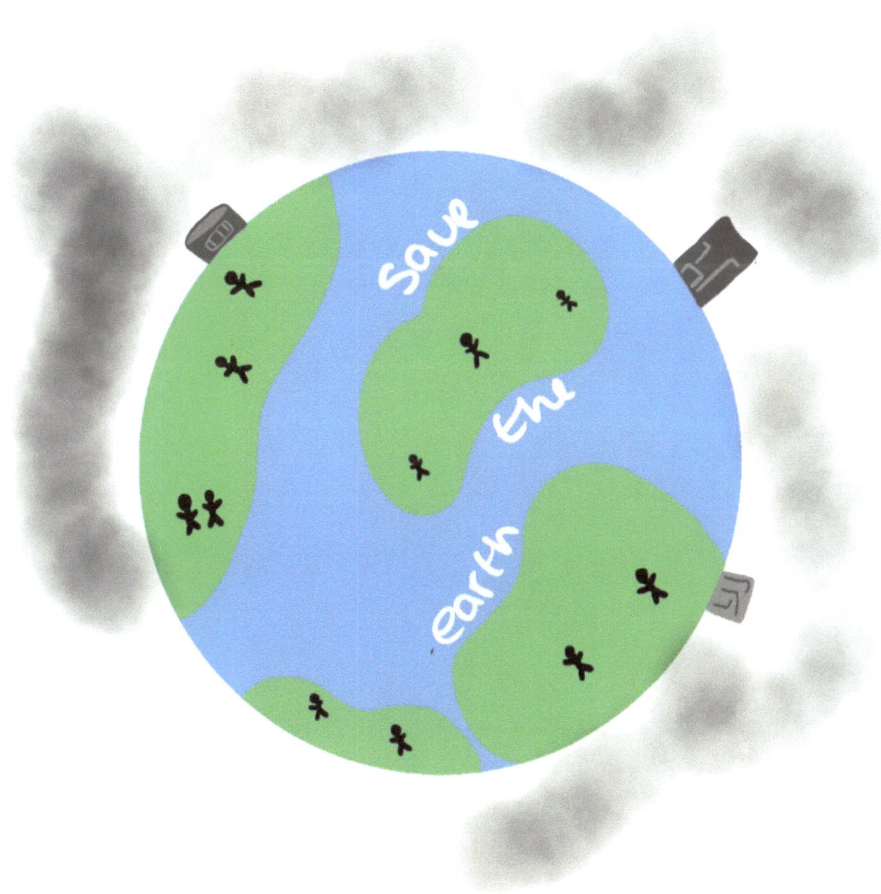

Black Lady with Blue Background

This print displays my love of using colors. This print represents a woman who is confident and intelligent. This creation is considered a favorite among my collection of art.

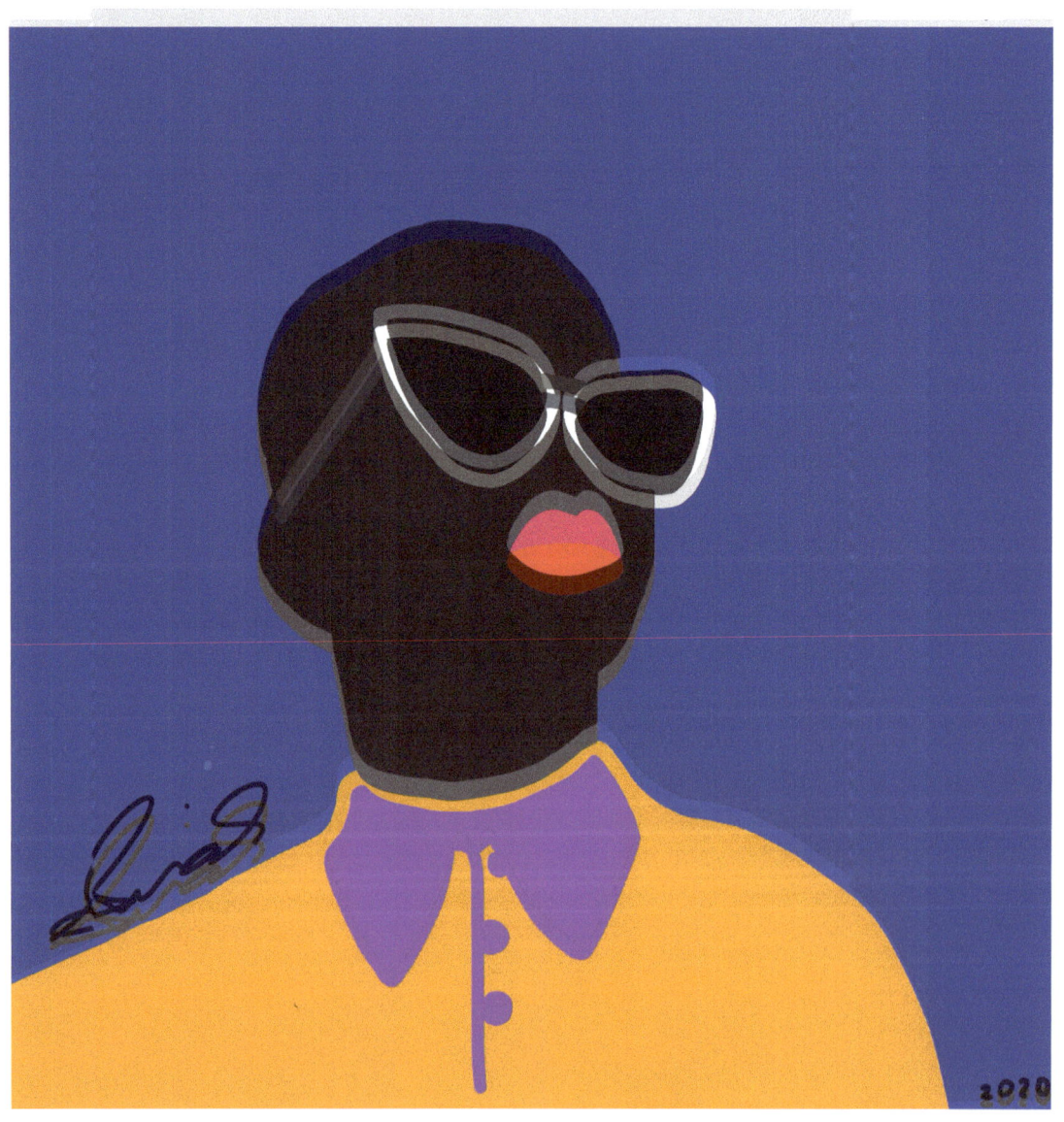

Veterans Strong

This print was suggested from one of my customers who is a veteran. He felt like I should represent veterans in my art. Thank you Veterans for your service.

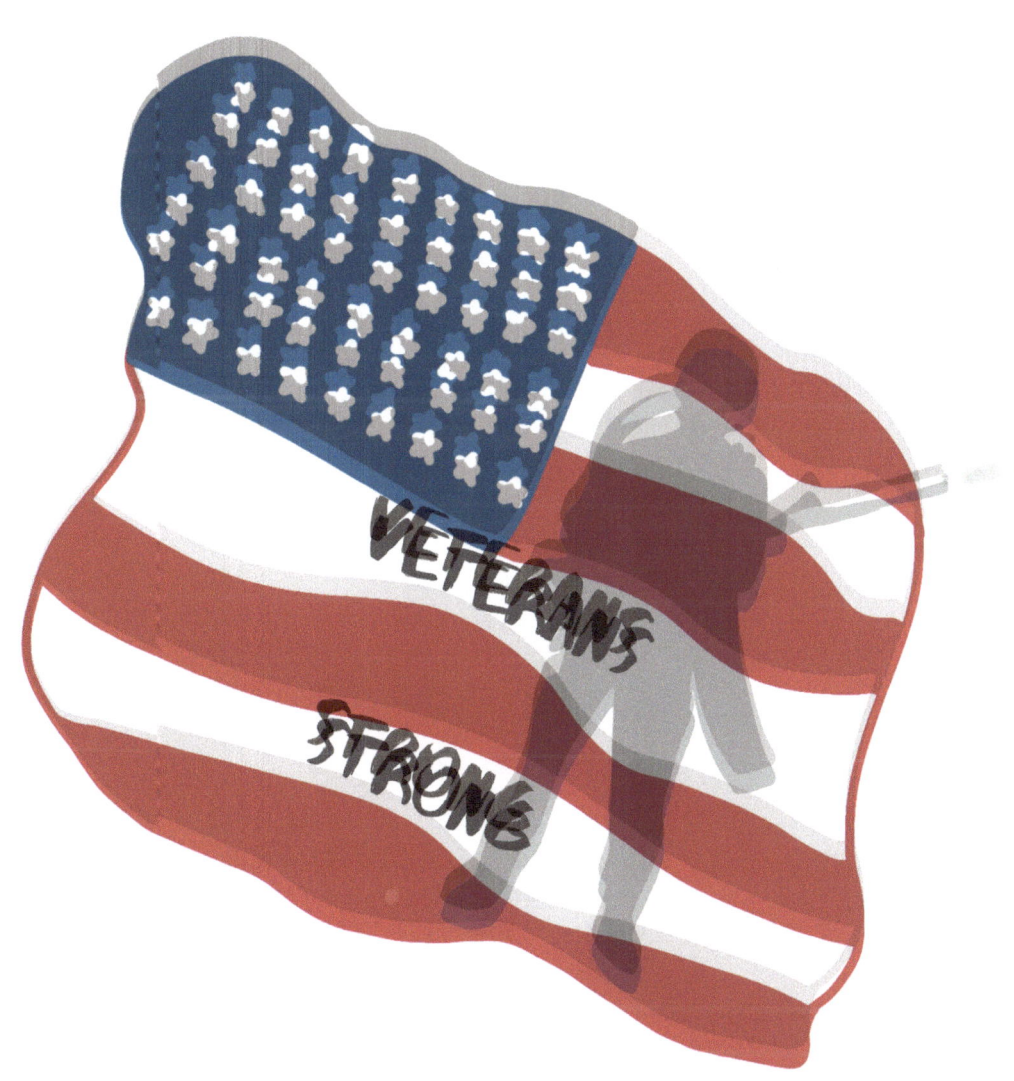

Black Man is A Man

This print is in honor of George Floyd and of all the African American men who have lost their lives to violence.

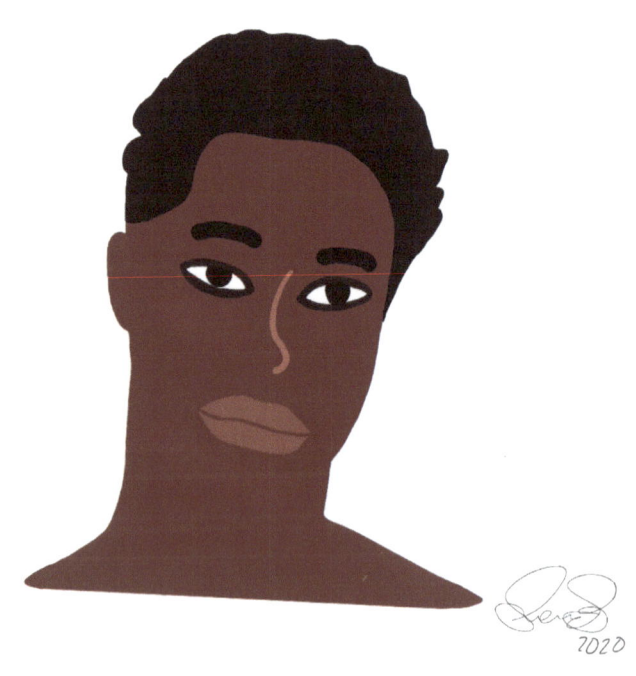

I Am Beautiful

This print represents a woman who is comfortable with being herself and seems to be thinking of something really important.

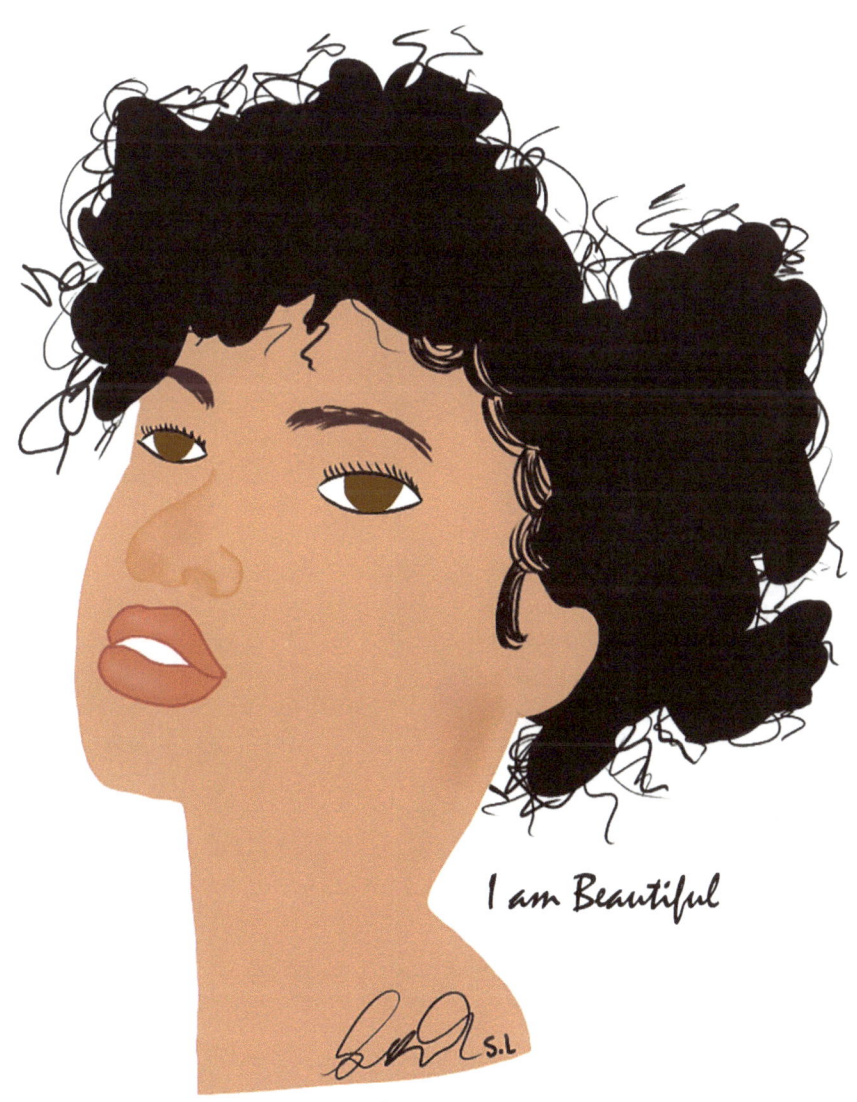

Brown Lady on a Blanket

I was inspired by a picture I saw on Pinterest of a lady sitting on the beach with an hat. This is a great decor for any office or home.

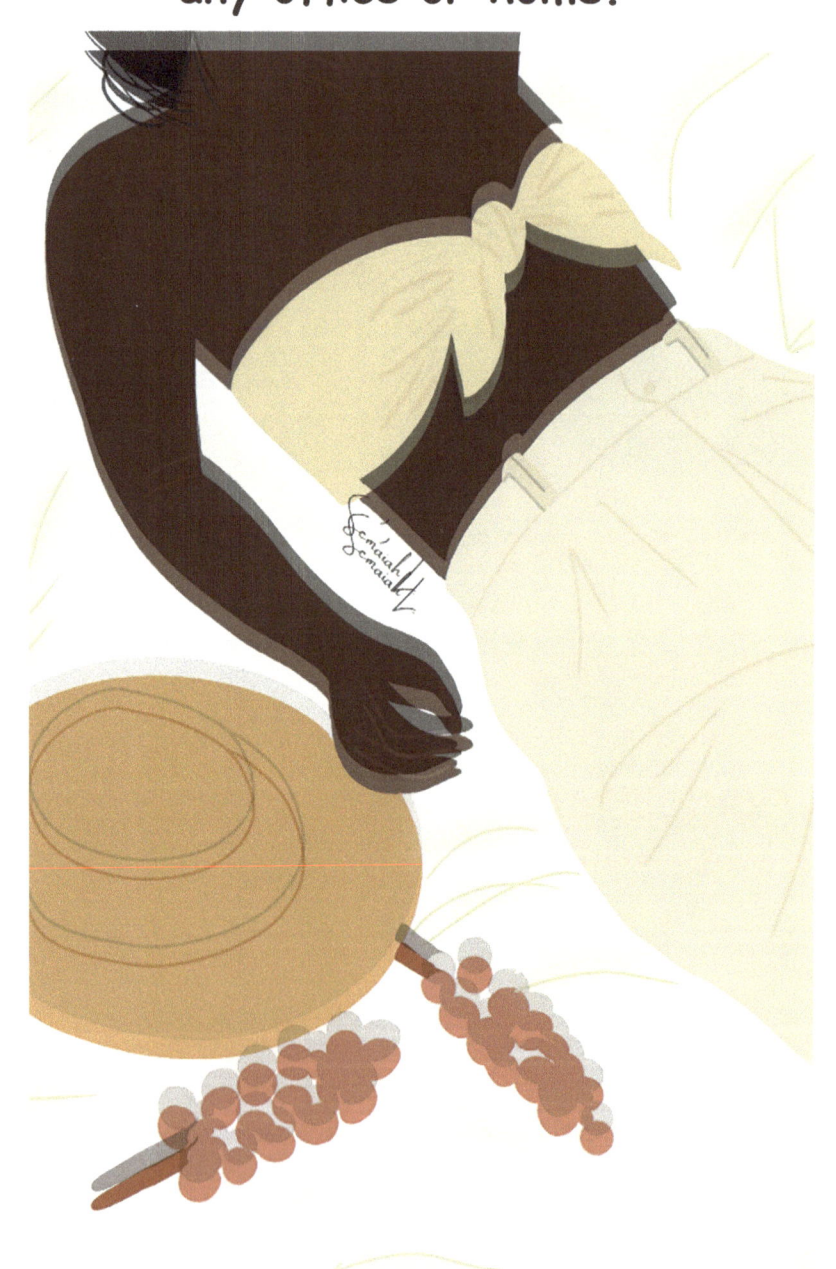

2020 Major Events

This print is inspired by people who was influential within our culture during the year of 2020. This picture includes Breonna Taylor, Donald Trump, Joe Biden, George Floyd, Chadwick Boseman and John Lewis.

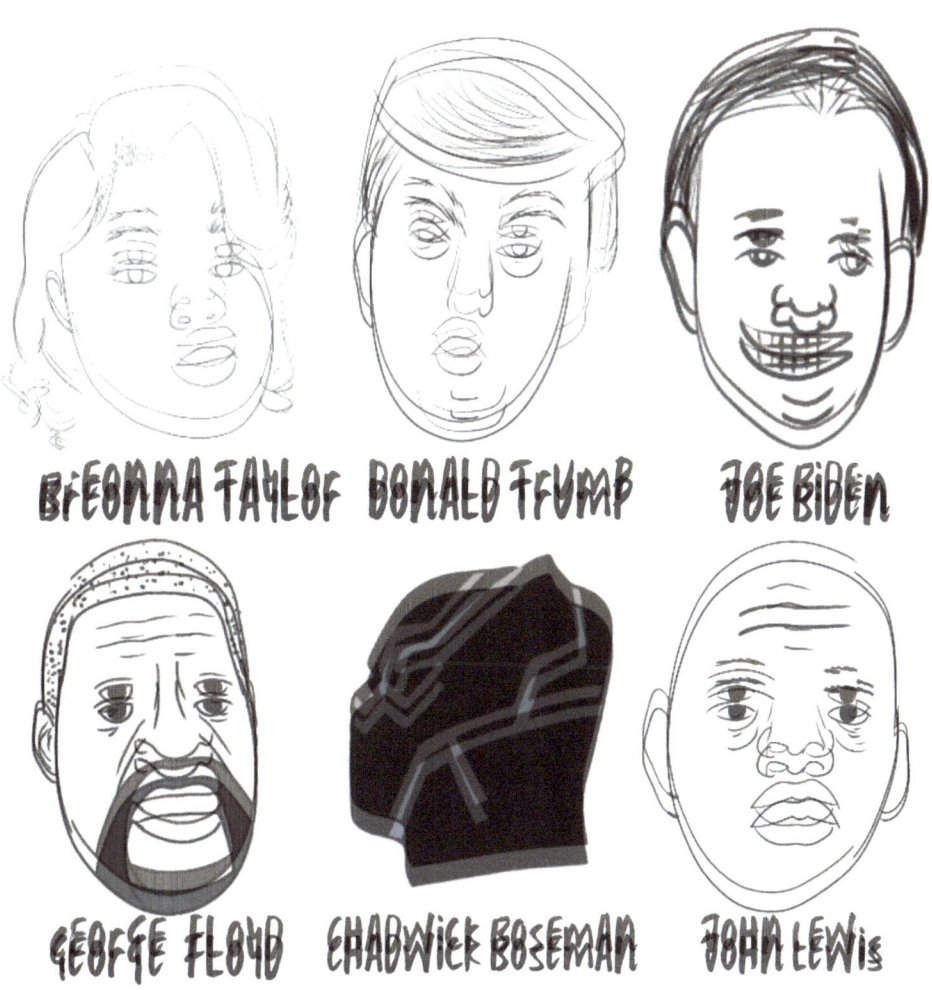

Beauty Queen

This print represents all the women of color who participate in beauty pageants.

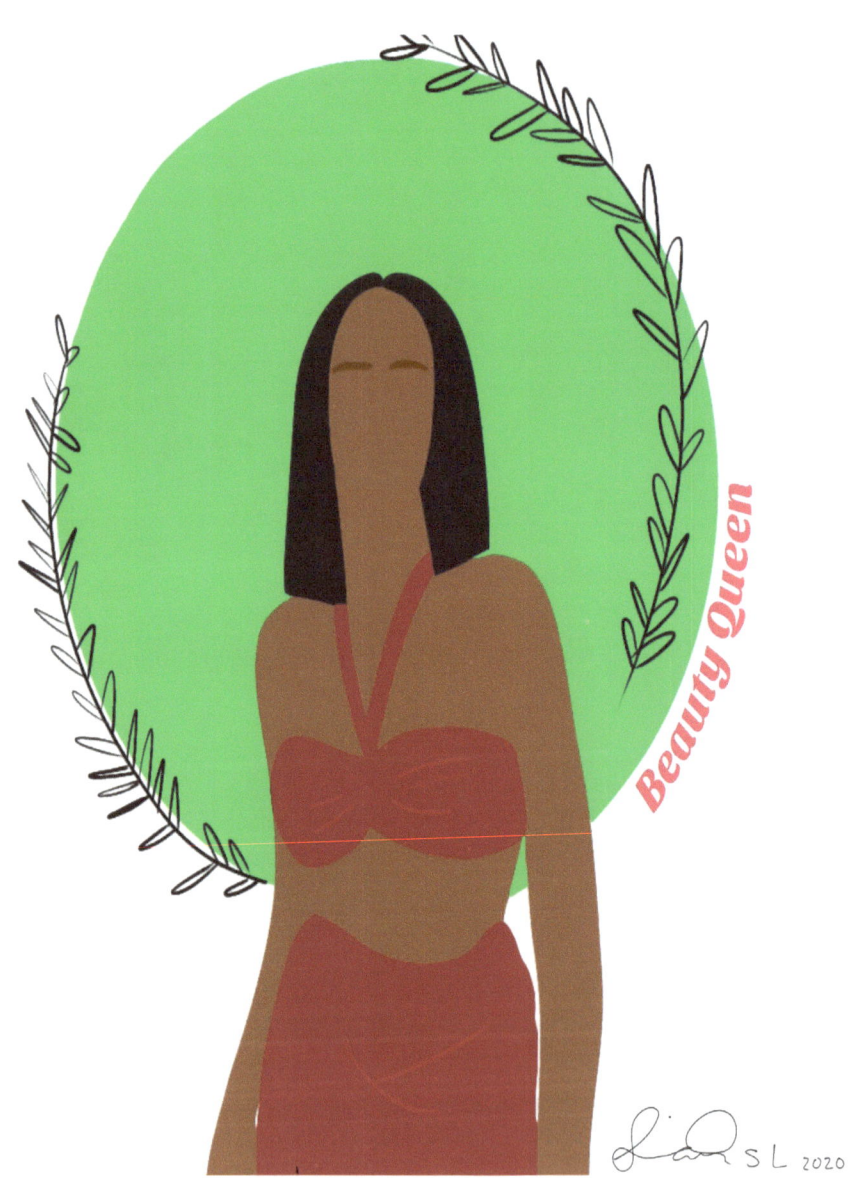

DIVA

This print was inspired by the boho aesthetic. I made a mix of browns because that is the main color of the boho theme.

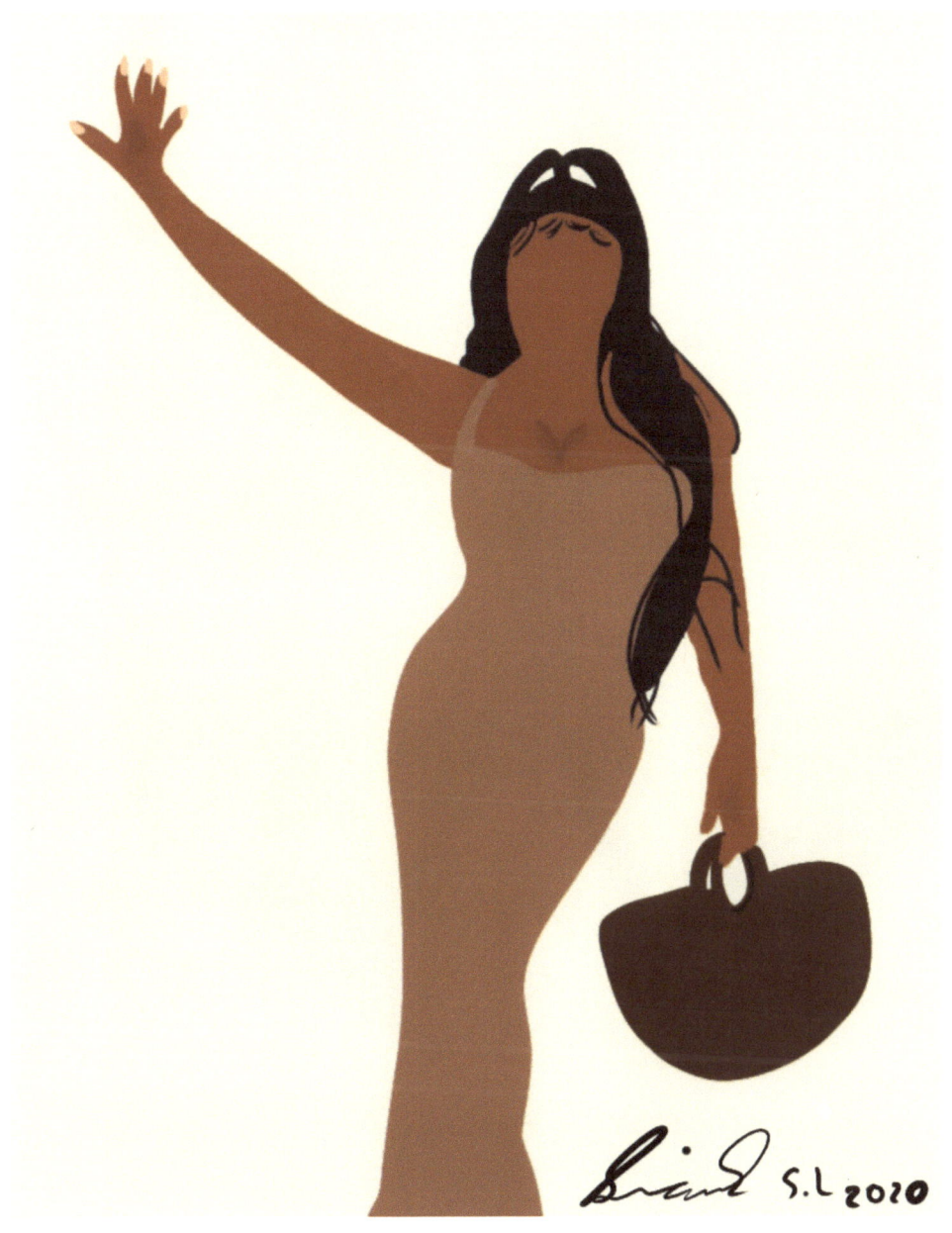

Fly High

This print has the word "Fly High" on it to inspire people to live their best lives and to work to achieve any desired goals.

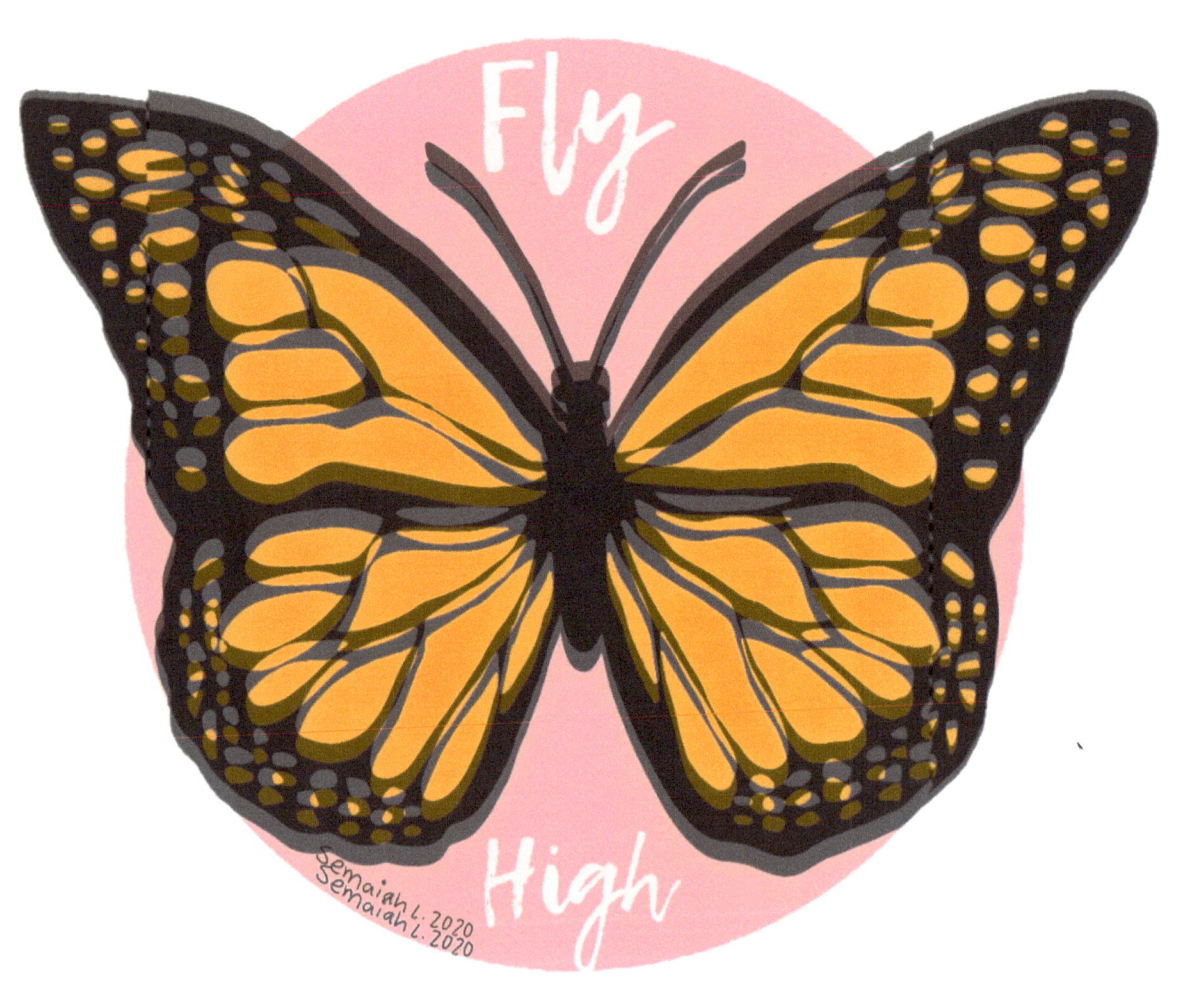

Flying Into Space

This print is inspired by my interest in tumblr aesthetic, space and galaxies.

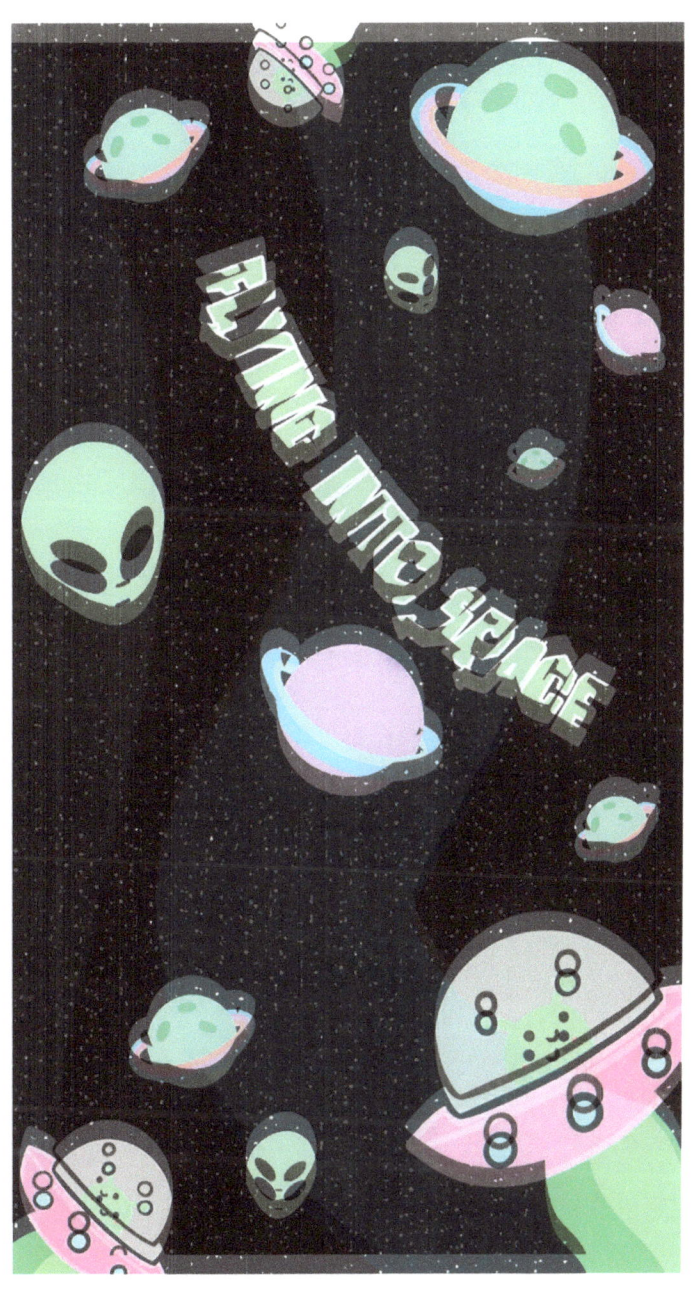

I Voted 2020 (Male)

The presidential election of 2020 was a very monumental election. This print represents all the African American men who voted for the first time.

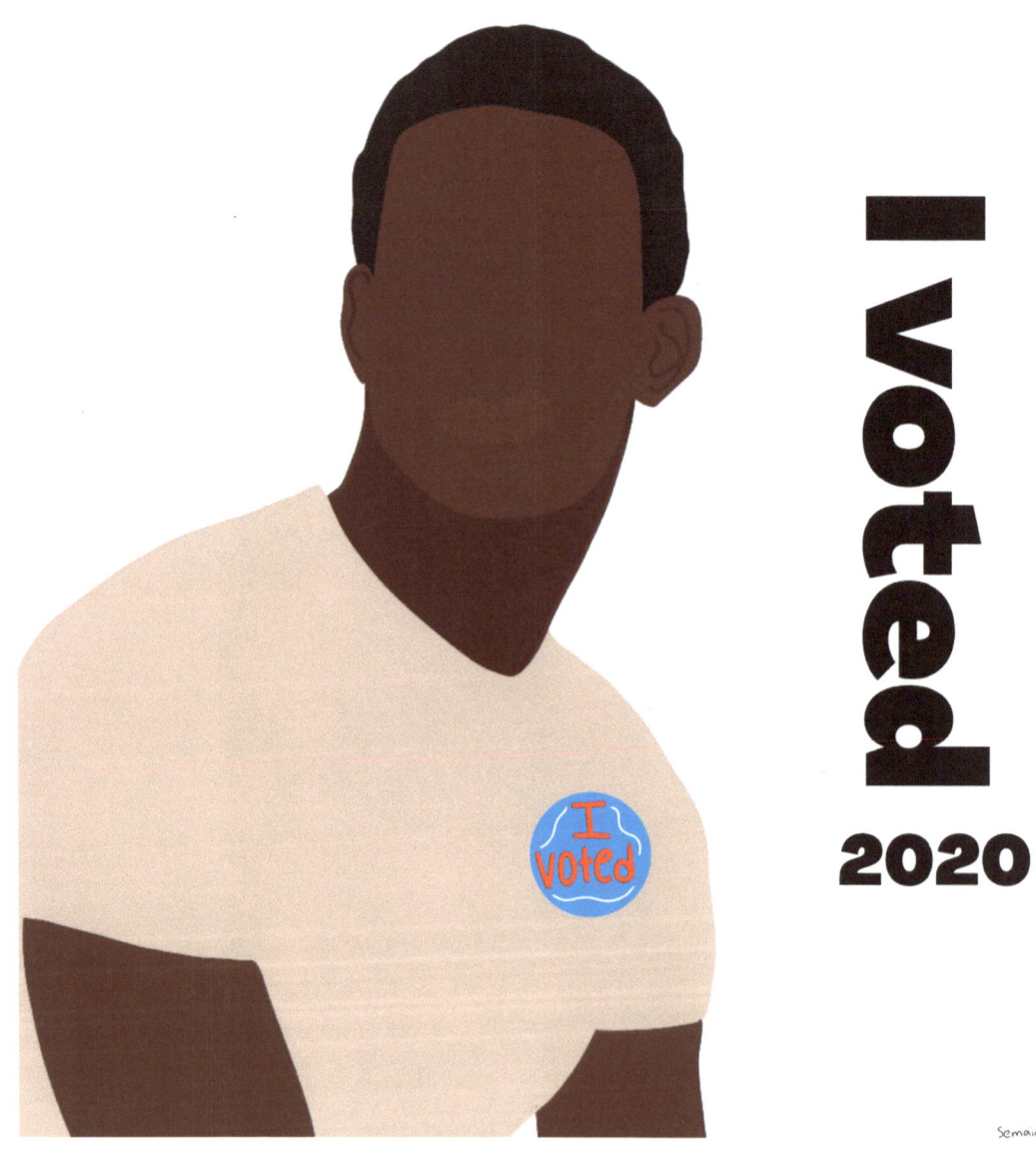

I Voted 2020 (Female)

The presidential election of 2020 was a very monumental election. This print represents all the African American women who voted for the first time.

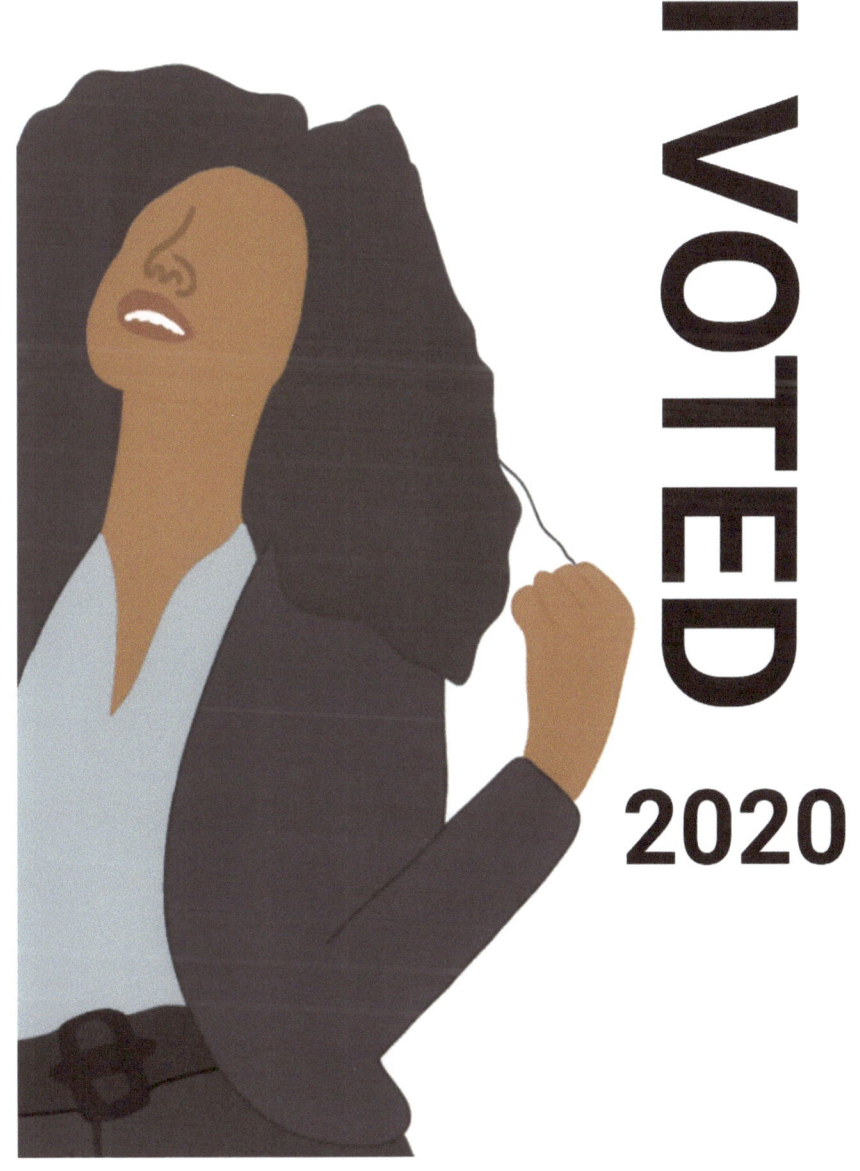

The Smell of Books

I was inspired by my love of reading books. This print is dedicated to all the book lovers.

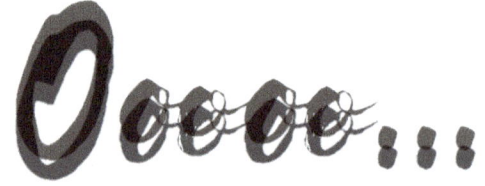

Amoung Us

This print was inspired by the popular game Amoung Us:

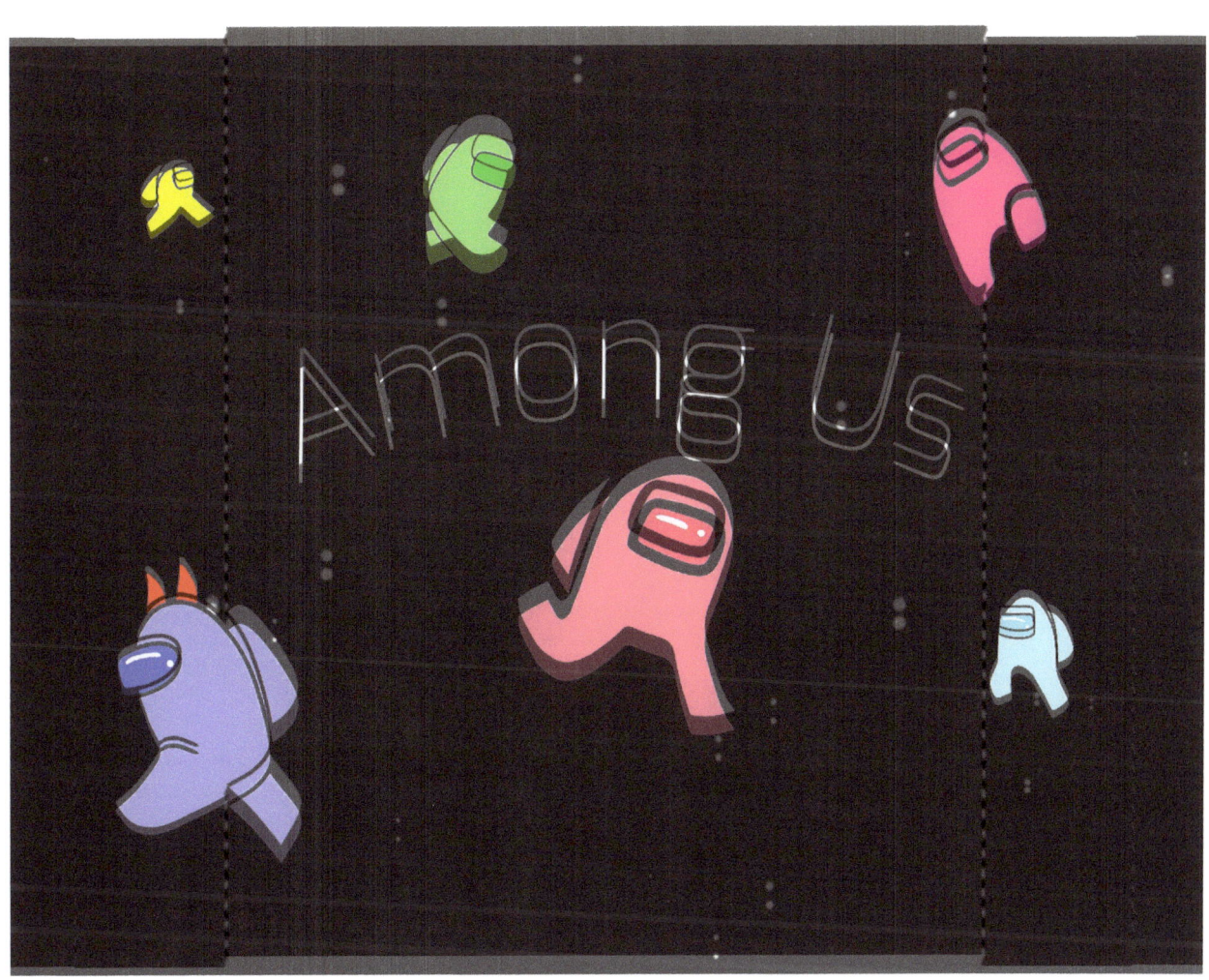

Holidays 2020

My mom inspired me to create this print to help celebrate the holidays. It took me awhile to decide to create this art. Eventually, I decided to create this art and it became a favorite to many during the holiday season.

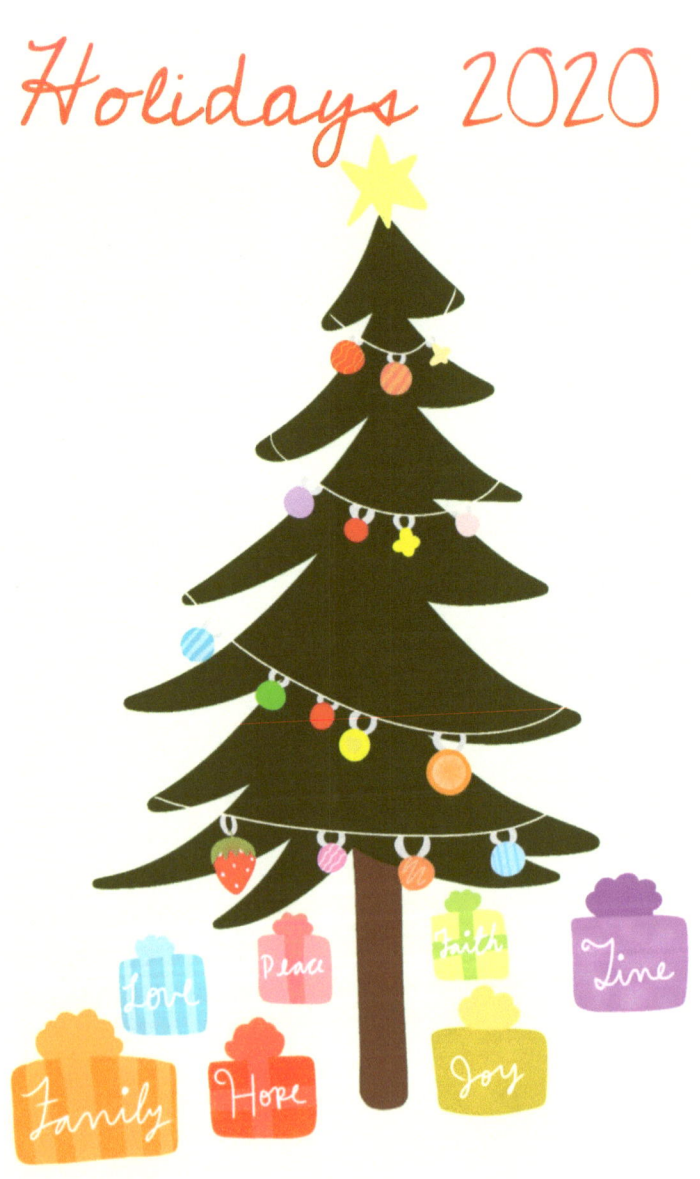

We Are All Beautiful Girls

This print represents all the girls that are my age or older that don't know they're beautiful. All girls are beautiful despite their body type or skin color. I normally draw pictures with just one person. I challenged myself to draw a picture with multiple people displayed within the art.

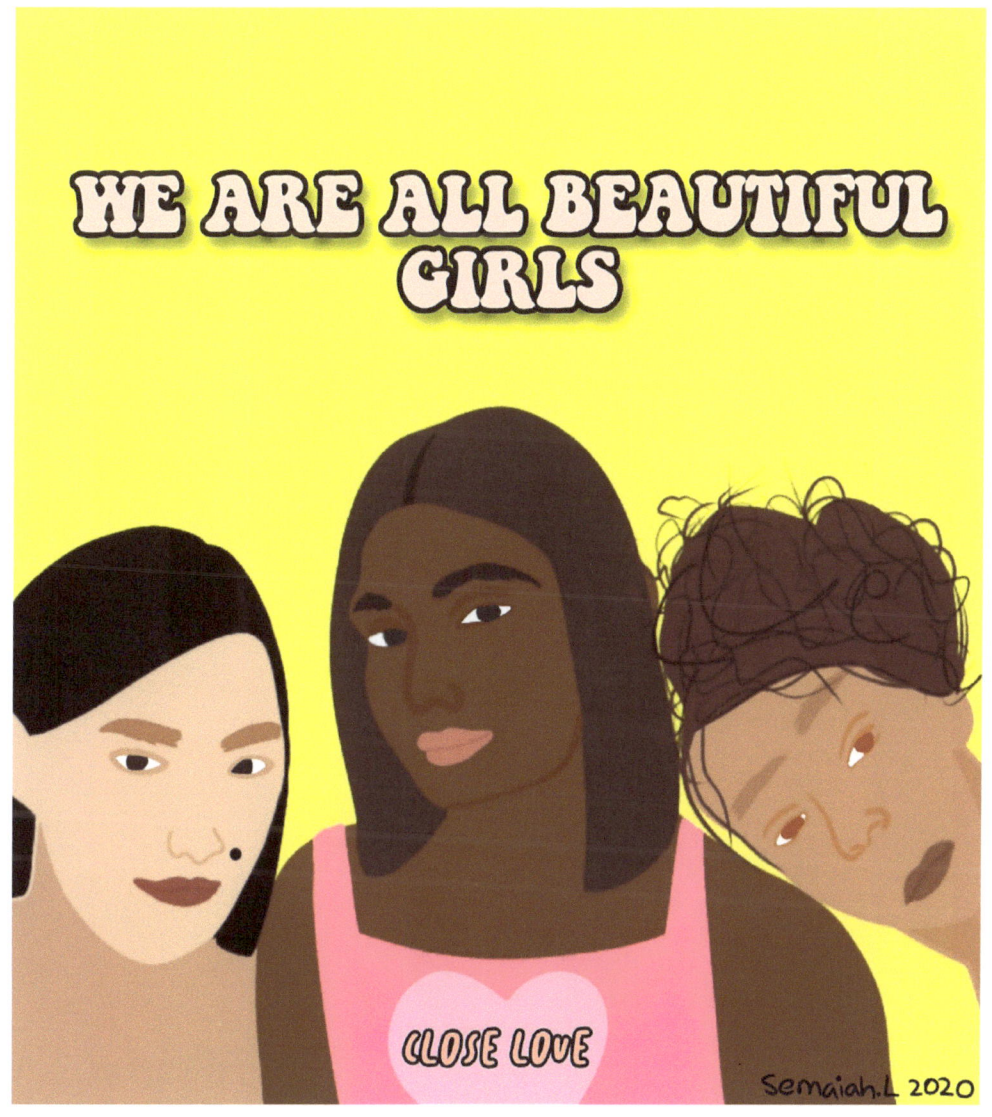

Bright Beauty

As the year 2020 ends, this picture represents a woman who is looking ahead and is looking forward to a better life in the year 2021. She is a survivor.

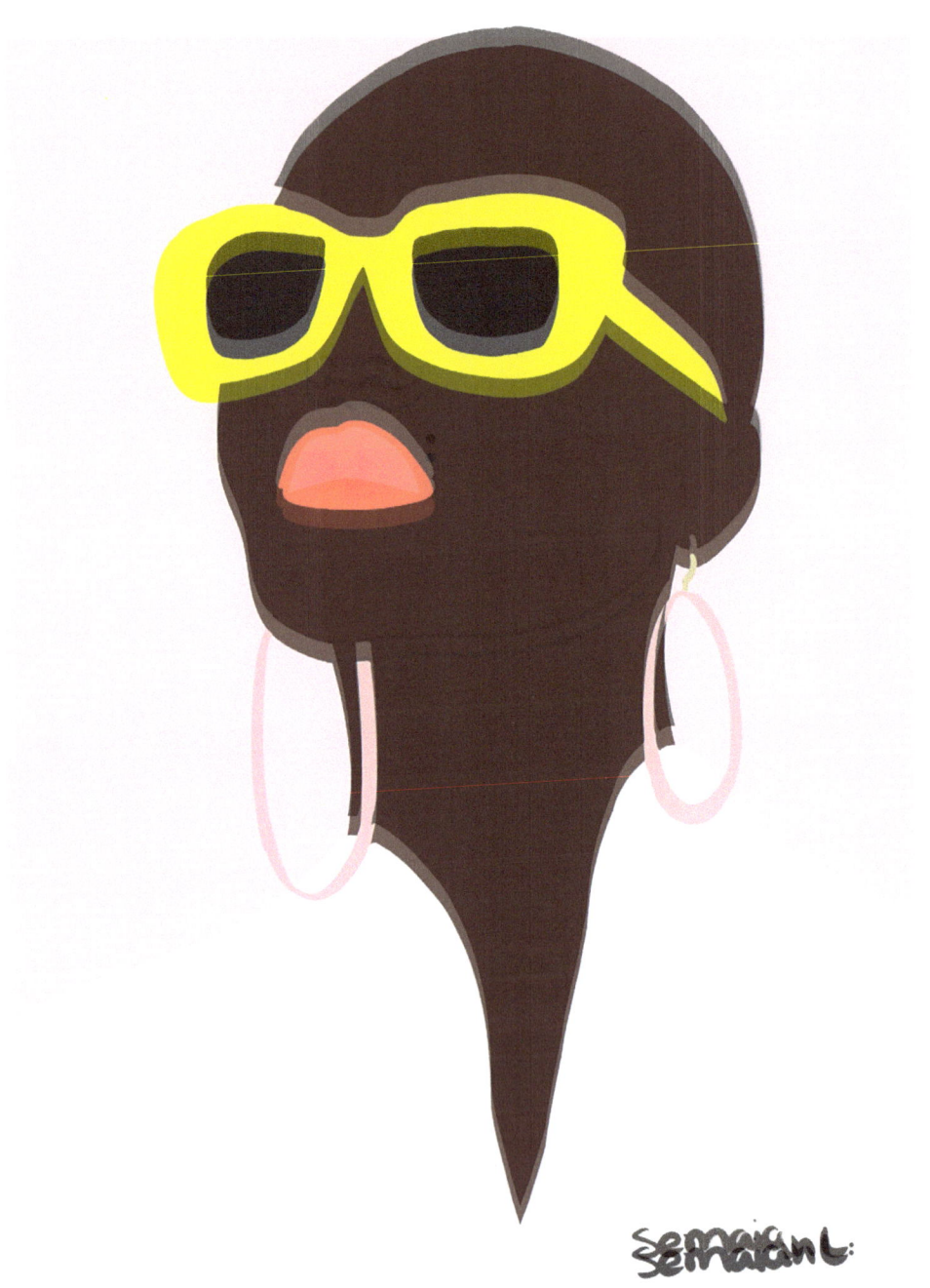

www.ingramcontent.com/pod-product-compliance
Lightning Source LLC
Chambersburg PA
CBHW051943210526
45473CB00006B/2356